"How are you?"
"I'm Fine."
Feelings Inside Never Expressed

Karsynn Icard

Humanity First Publishing—Rock Hill, SC
ISBN: 978-0-578-34014-2
Title: *How are You? I'm Fine. Feelings Inside Never Expressed*
Author: Karsynn Icard
Digital distribution | 2022
Paperback | 2022

Dedication

I dedicate this book to you. To the person who is wanting to break free from that still small voice that is telling you to remain silent. My hope is that you recognize you are a true force to be reckoned with. Your words carry so much power that have the ability to set this world, your world, on fire. In a world that is filled with so much heaviness, remain true to the softness that you were designed with and allow that to move you forward as you take on all that comes your way. You are the sun, so let all the light that is in you, flow through you, and continue to leave your forever needed mark.

I love that you are here.

From all the love in my heart,
Karsynn

Table of Content

But Why?

I realize you didn't do this to my life God.

However, you did allow it to happen. But I want to know; why?

Why are you allowing my family to suffer individually as well as a collective whole? Why did you allow me to lose three lives before their time?

Why did you allow me to witness death at such a young age?

Why do I feel like I can see freedom but I'm not close enough to touch it? Why do I feel pain? God: Because there is something I wired inside of you called; empathy. Empathy allows you to understand and share the feelings of another person. What breaks my heart, will break yours. This world is broken, it's breaking; constantly. I see it, I've lived it, I feel it. So can you.

Seeing families suffer, it breaks me.

Seeing fruit cast before its time, it breaks me. Seeing the death of a young boy drown, it broke me.

Conquering evil and seeing the victory I have for you wasn't easy, but it was worth it. And seeing that you can't see that yet, it breaks me.

Seeing you experience pain, it breaks me. This temporary home you're living in is not Heaven. That is why I tell you to set your mind on things above. Above, is where you will fully and wholeheartedly experience all the goodness I have saved for you.

1

Right now, your mission is people. It is each other. You were made to be relational. You were made to be communal. You were made to be real with one another. But instead, this is your human dialogue with one another.

"Hey, how are you?"

"I'm fine, and you?"

But let's take a moment and recognize what FINE stands for: Feelings Inside Never Expressed. What would your life look like if you started to break free from the voice that is telling you to stay silent?

It may start to look like this.

On July 17, 2021 on a Saturday afternoon, my Husband Matt and I walked into the hospital to release a life as a woman was simultaneously walking out who had just given birth to one. That moment will forever be one of the most painful and darkest moments I have yet to experience. I have experienced two miscarriages prior to this pregnancy but this was different. My baby was still alive inside of me, he/she was just growing in a spot that wouldn't sustain either of our lives. There is a 1% to 2% survival rate for a mom and her baby when this happens so you are presented with two options. You either remove one of your tubes or you receive an injection that releases the pregnancy. A decision I personally feel no mother, couple, or human being should have to make. For a week, I was searching for women who were me. I was trying to find anyone who can relate because everyone knows that when you are suffering, the only thing you want to feel and know is that you're not alone. I did not find as many women as I hoped so that is why I decided to speak up and break free from the voice that was telling me to stay silent. The voice that was telling me, "Don't expose yourself, after two miscarriages, and now this? What will people think of you?"

"Are you sure you made the right choice?"

"What is she doing wrong?"

But then, I realized I needed the next woman who may find herself searching for herself in others to know that she is not alone.

Your body is not broken. As much as you may believe that it is, it's not. We cannot keep allowing the enemy to make us feel shame for the experiences we have no control over and suffer in silence. We are not meant to carry the weight of the world and we most certainly are not meant to cover it up. We are human beings with feelings that deserve to be felt in its entirety. Since experiencing this particular pregnancy loss, my thoughts consisted of things like, "What's wrong with me?"

"How did I give birth to Lawson and now have three failed pregnancies?"

"Will I ever have kids again?"

"How is everyone around me able to have kids so easily and I can't?"

But that next morning after bringing my fears to God openly and honestly, I was reminded of these truths.

"Your baby was also the Lord's baby and sometimes he calls them home for a reason you won't know until you get into heaven."

"You will conceive again because the Lord has spoken life over you and not death."

"Your body is not broken, your mind is not weak, and your faith is not feeble. You just can't see it yet, but victory is around the corner."

Secondary infertility has brought some of the darkest moments into my life and Matt's, but our story is not over yet and neither is yours. Allow yourself to shatter because that's the only way you will heal. Don't put on a brave face if you don't want to. Be angry. Be frustrated. Be down, but while you are down know that when you do get back up, because you will. There will now be a Lioness heart and fire brewing inside of you that will not be crushed by the enemy's attempts to burn you. Your body is not broken. You are just proving to the darkness of this world that you can burn and still survive. You are fireproof and your story has just begun. Also, if you know someone who has experienced pregnancy loss and you don't know what to say or you can't find the right words, that's okay. There are no right words. Most likely, the person experiencing it doesn't know either. So release yourself from the pressure to find the right words and just be present and let them know you're there, whether that's physically, mentally, emotionally, or spiritually. There is something comforting about knowing that someone may not know exactly how you feel, but they do know what it feels like to experience sadness, anger, and pain because again, we are human beings and feelings are not meant to be shamed. So when you can exercise your ability to remember what those emotions feel like, it is easy to extend your human touch.

Or when all else fails, you can revert to letting them know you're ready to pick them up at anytime, take them to a secluded area and just scream, "F*** the enemy!" at the top of your lungs. Because, that is also healing.

Life is so hard and so complex that sometimes we just need to remind ourselves that we have been built to handle whatever happens next. I have found there to be so much freedom and not only freedom, but healing in vocalizing your pain. It does not have to be in front of anyone, it can even be through pen and paper. But get it out as many times as you need, to let the healing take place. I recognize that for many of us, our inner dialogue tells us that if we speak up or speak out we will be ridiculed and shamed for our truths, and to be honest, we very well may be. But here is the thing I have learned about following Christ. You start to see that you are in fact, made in his image. You are a light bearer and where there is light, darkness cannot survive. The perception that people have of you, is none of your business. People only shame you out of the brokenness of their own hearts and it hurts. We all have this deficiency, and why? Because we are human beings and human beings experience pain. It is inevitable, and the moment you realize that, you experience freedom. **You realize you are not the exception to the valleys of life.** The valley is what shapes you and shifts you into the person you're meant to become.

In 2016, I went to South Africa and on one of our days we went to a game park. For those that don't know, I have a very deep deep love for giraffes. I always have and I always will. So of course, the only animals I wanted to see were the giraffes. After driving around for an hour or so without seeing a single giraffe, I finally asked, "Where are the giraffes?!"

Our guide responded, "Oh you won't see the giraffes on the hill tops, you will find them in the valley because that is where the fruit is produced."

As those living in South Africa would say, "Shoo!" In that "aha" moment I was reminded that valleys are where the victors are born. "Shoo!" So if you find yourself in the valley, where I have been planted many times, please know that there is victory there. So sit in your valley a little while longer until what needs to take place is accomplished.

In closing of this chapter, I have written a tribute to all the Heaven-side mothers.

"You just had a miscarriage. Do you understand what has happened?"

Two sentences, eleven words, one statement… in a single moment, it all stops.

Picturing you meeting your baby for the first time. It stops. Seeing your family light up when they hold your baby for the first time, it stops. Imagining your children playing together, it stops. Wondering will they take after you or your partner, it stops. Your imagination, your sense of wonder…it all just stops.

Two sentences, eleven words, one statement… in a single moment, it all stops.

I used to believe that grief began the moment you acknowledged what has happened to you; I was wrong. Grief begins the moment you realize what could have been, no longer is… grief begins the moment a piece of your world ends whether you can fully comprehend that or not.

Life often hands us situations that we are not equipped for; but given the right space to process each and every moment, healing is attainable.

On three different occasions, I have grieved what it means for it all to stop...and if you have found yourself in a similar situation, then I wrote this for you. I wrote this for us.

To the Woman who Mothers not earth side but heaven side...

It hurts. It does not just hurt, it feels empty, it feels numbing. How can you miss someone so much that you have never even met? Except, wait...you have. They were a part of you. They knew who you were from the inside ... and isn't that what matters most? Your inner being? The purest and truest part of you. Twenty-seven days, eight weeks, four months, nine months...it does not matter how long your baby was with you. They were with you long enough for you to imagine your life earth side with them. Long enough for you to know that your life would forever be changed by this little piece of heaven.

But what happens when God decides to bring them back to heaven before you are ready?

To the woman who mothers not earth side but heaven side...It hurts, it does not just hurt, it feels empty, it feels numbing. It feels like your body failed you at the one thing it was designed to do. Bring life. But you did bring life and brought it long enough to make a difference, whether in your life or those you find close to you. You brought life long enough for it to mean something. Your body did not fail you; you are not broken.

To live on earth but have a part of you in heaven is an out of body feeling that I would not wish for anyone, but for the one who has; Your body did not fail you, you are not broken. You gave Heaven what it needed most, your heart. To the woman who mothers not earth side but heaven side...I am you, you are me. We are one.

& we are not alone.

Sending love,
    Karsynn Icard

Cultivating Rest with a Weary Soul

I was having a conversation with one of my siblings one day and they made the statement, "I just want to know that everything is going to be okay. And that I will have what it takes to create again."

I realized that although we were experiencing different struggles, we found ourselves in a similar season. As you get older, you realize that you may not always be able to operate in the same way that you once did, and that is a hard truth to accept. It's almost like you are on a waitlist at your favorite restaurant and you finally get called that your reservation became open. So you arrive at the restaurant knowing exactly what you are going to order because for months you had been waiting for this experience. You get seated, and they bring out a sample of the dish for you to try to confirm that that's what you still want. It tastes SOOO good. Then some time goes by and they come back saying that the dish is no longer available and they're not sure when they will be able to put it back on the menu. I know that may seem like a silly way to put it, but it feels like an immediate closed door and zero closure. For me, it was receiving an injection that altered who I once was in order to save who I am now. It was recognizing how traumatizing my past experience and current experiences have been and not knowing how to move forward. It was feeling helpless like everyone was now looking at me for my wounds and not my victories. Feeling like where you once fit in, you no longer do.

If you have found yourself in a similar season, hear me when I say this. You are a trailblazer. Do not for one second feel ashamed by your current or past narrative. Use your experience to create an atmosphere of openness and freedom for others. In doing so, you will allow people to do the same that come behind you, who find themselves feeling like they won't end up where they thought they always would. By creating this atmosphere and allowing others to hear your words and share your fight, they will know that all things are possible. In times of weariness, God has given us just enough energy for that day or task at hand. Relax knowing that not everything needs to be accomplished before the sun goes down. Learn to cultivate grace and patience for yourself. When you do, you will look back on this season and remember the tenderness you gave yourself and miss those moments of stillness. You are in the fire, but you can burn and still survive.

I was in Arizona one time visiting my best friend and we were on a mountain tour when our jeep guide said to us, "Did you know that fires are actually nature's way of resetting? In fact, pine trees won't take root unless they burn."

You may be surrounded by a fire in your life but there is also a fire inside of you that the Lord has placed as a way to restructure and reroot yourself into his unwavering goodness. We are not here to live a life of passivity, but of courage and unshakeable peace. **There is peace and then there is supernatural**

10

peace. Human peace consists of calming the mind and relaxing the body. But supernatural peace is a peace only God can give. It is a peace that surpasses all understanding of human wiring and in order to obtain that peace, you have to be still. You have to stop berating and belittling yourself mentally and emotionally, sink below the surface, and feel the fire. Within that fire, is a light that the Lord will use to guide you. So in closing of this chapter, know that everything will be okay and you will create again in the way that you have uniquely been designed. I know this because when you walk in tandem with the Lord he has the last word and in his word he says, "I have begun a good work in you and will bring it to completion."

Affirmation: "I openly bring my honest and weary soul to the forefront of my life, but this is not the end for me. God has the last and final word over my life."

Managing Mental Health as a Mama

There is so much that goes into Motherhood. You are now looking at life through the lens of everything that has happened to you up until that point. No matter which path you took to Motherhood; whether that path was fostering, adoption, surrogacy or getting pregnant, growing life inside of you, and then birthing that life, you are a Mama, and that can be beautiful and challenging all at the same time. Now you are taking on the role of maintaining that life which can bring on overwhelming emotions and a looming weight and worry that you don't know how to combat.

Something I recently learned was, you cannot outgrow worry. If you are anything like me, or even just a human being at that, we all have things we worry about. We worry about the things that have happened in the past and how they may affect our tomorrow; we worry about the things that are happening in the moment and how they are going to play out, and we even create these potential situations of what "could" happen and how we will potentially feel. We worry about our future, our friends, our families, etc. You name it, and someone in the world is worrying about it. Prior to learning about worry, I felt like if I prayed long enough, meditated long enough, captivated my thoughts long enough, I could overcome worry. You will never conquer worry, because it is a part of the flesh. By that I mean, it will always be a part of who we are, so to fight it is to be expending energy that we could be preserving. I am continuing to learn that **it is not about overcoming worry, but coming out of worry.** I now realize all the strategies I have been implementing are healthy and beneficial; but it is not the longevity of their practice in which I will reap the benefits, it is in the consistency of pointing myself back to Christ every single time worry makes its way into my head and heart. It is in learning and leaning on Christ to trust him and what he says. It is the practice of recognizing I am operating in the flesh and in that very moment, stepping outside of myself and habitual thoughts of worry and trusting that God has seen my yesterday, my today, and my tomorrow and all the remaining days of my life.

So simply say, "God, I rest in you. I lay these thoughts to rest because they are not serving me with the peace you have made available to me."

Which brings me to my next phase of livelihood and motherhood; our bodies. Our bodies are the one piece of ourselves that we came into this world with and the one part that will carry us to the very end. What we experience mentally, our bodies are experiencing physically.

The trauma, the physical pain, the exhaustion, and the weight of all of life's transitions. Something I really struggled with and currently struggle with are night feedings. Knowing that our bodies require rest to reset and replenish, early motherhood requires broken sleep and active participation regardless of the hour. Yet, when my mind doesn't want to do it, my body will. When I hear Lawson cry, as much as I want to stay put, I get up and so do you. Our bodies fight for us even when we don't feel it. And because of that, we should take more time to acknowledge and celebrate all that our bodies have accomplished and continue to accomplish on our behalf. Our bodies have been impacted by some of our hardest battles yet this is the first thing we choose to berate.

We think things like, "I wish you looked different, I wish you would smooth out here, or add some weight here, or thin out here. I wish you would have clearer skin in this area. Be darker here. Be lighter here. I wish you could fit in that, but you can't. Ugh. I hate this. I wish, I wish, I wish."

Meanwhile, our bodies just stay silent and take it. Every single time. And the crazy thing is, they wake up the next day, still serving us. Still fighting for us. It's sad to think about when I catch myself doing this. Beating up the one thing that has been my most loyal companion all these years. You do know that there was a time where we did love our bodies, right? **We loved them before someone else told us we shouldn't.**

Before we were conditioned to believe that what we hold in ourselves is not enough. In my experience with pregnancy + postpartum, my thoughts towards my postpartum body have been my hardest battle to combat. I found myself constantly hoping my body would go back to what it was, but now I'm learning to hope and strive towards my body going back to something that I once loved. To love the skin that has set me apart from others and simultaneously kept me close with another. To love the parts of me that have walked in rooms that changed my life. To love the things my body has allowed me to see, hear, taste, smell and my favorite, touch. To experience human touch is to experience life and our bodies have given us the gift of that experience. There are so many experiences that we can name that our bodies have allowed for us and I wonder what it would look like if we started to appreciate that.

Also, as I continue to share from my personal experience of motherhood, I want to mention that everyone's experiences are different and unique to them. No journey of motherhood looks the exact same for everyone and I think that is also something to remember, so take the pressure off to perform and 'mother' in a way that those around you may be caring for their family. The child and/or children that have been placed under your care have been placed there with intention. You are the only mom in this world that can love and care for your baby in a way that your baby needs. That is freeing. There is not another soul out there like yours who can give love to your child the way you do so hold on to that truth when you start to doubt your efforts.

Managing mental health is so complex, and in my experience, managing mental health as a mom is a complex fight. I was listening to a talk one day given by a Trauma Therapist, and she shared pieces of wisdom that I will never forget. She was speaking about feelings and she talked about 'the conflict of duality.'

She said, "This is how we feel - we don't feel like we can be grateful for what we have and be honest at the same time."

For me, that encompassed all things motherhood. You can't say, "I am grateful for my child/children but I am drained." Because then that comes across as being ungrateful.

You can't say, "I enjoy being able to breastfeed but it is taking everything out of me." Because there are mothers all around the world who would kill to be in your position. So again, ungrateful. The list could go on but in her talk she made a statement that I loved. She gave an example regarding spirituality.

She said, "Can I admit I'm anxious or sad about this and does that mean I am spiritually immature? Yes, two things can be true. I can be excited about accepting Jesus into my life but I can also mourn that God will ask me to do hard things."

We have conditioned ourselves to believe that there can only be one truth in our lives. Either you love it, or you don't. Either you trust God or you don't. Either you are happy or you're sad. But let me tell you, being a human being is so complex. Two things can be true about you. You can love motherhood and still miss your previous life. You can love being a stay at home mom and still wish you had a job to "clock out of". You can love being a working mom and still wish you could solely stay home with your child/children. Two things can remain true in your life. There is so much freedom in breaking free from the voice that tells you it has to be one or the other but it doesn't. Allow yourself the opportunity to hold space for grief and gratitude, and in doing that you make room for what is necessary. To feel. And to feel it in its entirety.

Let's go back to the complexities of managing your mental health as a mom. You are a giver, you are a leader, you are a lover, and you are a lifeline. But for the sake of your mental capacity, taking a break from time to time is needed. You don't have to prove to yourself or anyone just how well you can manage motherhood. Your new way of living will take time. You are now a refined version of yourself; wiser, stronger, more intuitive, and resilient than ever before. You are experiencing growth and that is a beautiful thing. So give yourself time to grow and give yourself space to exist just the way you are. It is going to be okay.

Finish this sentence, "I want to teach my kids what it means to be brave, and to me, being brave means...."

_____

_____

_____

_____

_____

_____

_____

_____

_____

_____

_____

Be the Flower that Rises through the Concrete

Isn't it crazy how you can believe in the impossible for someone else, but you can't for your own life? Why is that? Is it because you feel like you've been knocked down so many times that at this point it's just easier to stay down? It's easier to not get your hopes up and set your expectations too high because you've been let down too many times? I mean, I get it. That makes sense. When you see a pattern of road blocks and u-turns it's hard to imagine a freeway of freedom.

But here is the wild part. Here is the paradox. Your fight fuels the impossible. When did we stop believing in miracles? Because last time I checked, miracles are what God does best. I truly believe that there is a part in each and every one of us deep down that still believes in magical moments. A part of us that still believes despite all the turmoil in the world, it is the wildflowers that remain through it all. Be the wildflower that rises through the concrete.

Be the soul that changes the trajectory of life by believing in the impossible. Because when you do, you might just be surprised at what experiences are waiting for you. You want to know the secret for believing in the impossible? Lean in now... a little closer... okay, here it is.

Believe that God can do far more through you than you could ever imagine. Break free from the voice that is telling you that you have to be your own savior. You absolutely do not. So stop trying. Be the clay, not the clay maker.

If you're reading this, that means there is still air inside of your lungs. It means there is still a mission for your life with your name on it. A mission that has yet to be completed. There is a specific purpose that is awaiting your touch, your thoughtfulness, and your magic; and guess what? It's not going anywhere. One more thing we need to learn to break free from is, feeling like the plan for our life has an expiration date on it. The experiences you're meant to have, the journey you're meant to take, it will happen for you. Why? Because what is meant for you and only you cannot be taken from you.

No matter how hard society tries to make you believe, "You have to do it, and you have to do it now!" It is just not true. There is nothing in the world, not even society that has the power to take away God's gift and purpose that he's put on your life. So breathe.

The difficulties you find yourself in that are weighing you down cannot stop the calling that is already on your life.

Be the flower. Be the flower that rises through the concrete.

If you had to believe in the impossible in one area of your life, what would it be?

_____

_____

_____

_____

_____

_____

_____

_____

_____

_____

_____

_____

_____

_____

_____

_____

_____

_____

_____

_____

_____

_____

Your Melanin is Magical

Specific chapter for the BIPOC community - Black Indigenous People of Color, the way you take up space in this world is absolutely breathtaking.

As a person of color, especially as a woman of color, I have always felt lesser than. Like I needed to somehow prove my worthiness in a room full of people who did not look like me. I felt like I needed to be the one who moved aside when walking down the sidewalk, the one who kept quiet, kept the peace, and made sure no one noticed that I was there as a way to say, "don't worry I'm safe."

But I have come to realize, my melanin, your melanin, is what makes us magical. We are so much more than entertainment on a screen or a good time on the dance floor. We have been conditioned to believe that we will be accepted and loved when our hair is straight, our words are few, and our contributions are behind closed doors.

No lover, it is time for you to stop looking at your skin as a by-product of your existence and time to step into your magically, hand-crafted skin. Rise up to show the world that you are so much more than what they give you credit for. Your native tongue is a melody that soothes the soul, your roots run deep into the soil that your ancestors curated, and you come from a lineage of kings and queens.

Your Melanin is what makes you magical. So stand in your truth.

We are innovators, we are educators, we are role models, we are powerful, we are universal, and we are resilient.

Our Melanin IS MAGICAL.

We cannot be placed in a box and wrapped with white ribbon. So let your hair speak of its unmatched beauty, let your soul speak of its strength, and let your voice speak of its power. **No one holds the key to your cage, but you.** It is time to fly and show the world that you are so much more than what you are given credit for.

Affirmation: "The unique design of who I am is worthy of taking up space in this world. I will not allow fear to be a part of my story, I will inhale peace and exhale love. Always, love."

It May Not Seem Like it, but I See You

For whatever reason, there are certain things we feel the need to keep hidden. It may be because we know if we break our silence, we will be shamed, or judged, or even abandoned. So we suffer in silence and hold some of the deepest parts of us close enough to almost kill us.

Well, it may not seem like it, but I see you. To the person who wakes up every day fighting for their life with just enough courage to step outside for five minutes and then crawl back to bed, I see you.

To the person who is working overtime just to keep a roof over their family's head, I see you.

To the person who is too afraid to show their family and friends who they really are, I see you.

To the person who continuously gives love without receiving it in return, I see you.

To the sibling who takes on the role of a parent, I see you.

To the person who doesn't know if what they are doing is what they are supposed to be doing with their life, I see you.

To the person who never gives up hope and to the person who currently has none, I see you. It may not seem like it, but I see you.

Your efforts are not in vain. Your attempts are not without cause. Your value is not determined by your current season of life and your worth is not found in those you surround yourself with.

You are a human being with emotion. **You are a human being that has and will continue to leave a mark on this earth just by existing just as you are.** One thing we as humans never worry about, is the sun not rising the next day. We never go to bed anxious thinking, "Is the sun going to forget to rise tomorrow?"

If the same God who created the sun, the moon and all the stars, has also breathed life into you, then not only will he make the sun rise on your behalf but he will bring light to all the dark areas of your life without hesitation. So whatever is making you anxious right now, believe that just as the sun will rise tomorrow, your life will accomplish all that it needs to in the timing that it needs to.

Your efforts are not in vain, your attempts are not without cause and your value is not determined by your current season.

It may not seem like it, but I see you.

What are three areas of your life that you wish people could truly see?

_____

_____

_____

_____

_____

_____

_____

_____

_____

_____

_____

_____

_____

_____

_____

_____

_____

_____

_____

_____

_____

_____

_____

_____

A Letter from:
Me to You

If you gain nothing else from this short book, I hope you gain this. The next time someone asks you how you really are, I hope you have the courage to answer with honesty, transparency, and openness. I hope you recognize that your words matter to the world and the words that are shared with you should be held with grace and compassion.

Surviving is hard. But surviving while staying silent is even harder. You were never meant to stay shackled to the voice that is telling you to stay silent about the emotions that are taking place in your soul. Your words are your truth so I pray that you have the courage to speak your truth with your whole heart.

Secondly, I hope you realize that at this moment, you are deeply valued by the writer of this book. I have prayed for you and I have prayed over you. The parts of you that you have left unseen should receive just as much care as the parts of you that you allow to be exposed.

Thirdly, if you find yourself in a season of desiring more than what you are currently experiencing then this is my hope for you: I hope you never correlate God's lack of movement in your life to the severity of your prayers.

Oftentimes, when we don't see God move or we don't see a shift that we have so fervently pushed towards we think it is because of our lacking.

We have thoughts like, "Maybe I didn't pray hard enough?"

"Maybe I didn't believe as hard as I should've?"

Or even worse, we cast judgments like, "Well did you pray hard enough?"

"You just need to have more faith."

A friend of mine once shared a very simple prayer with me in the midst of a dark and hopeless season that held so much more power than I had anticipated. She said, "Karsynn, sometimes the only thing I can pray is, 'Lord, help my unbelief.'"

I want you to know that God does not base how He will answer your prayers by the intensity or longevity of your prayers. I am a firm believer that as much as He loves to hear the details of your desires and the length of your conversations He equally values your simple yet powerful prayers. Such as, "Lord, help my unbelief."

So for the person who has and is believing God for more but hasn't seen Him move in the way you had hoped, does not mean you did not pray hard enough or long enough. It simply means that right now, His way is better for you and ultimately for his glory. What the enemy intends for evil God turns it for His good. So don't think for one second that because you can't see the victory yet your prayers weren't good enough. If you brought them to the Lord with an open and vulnerable heart, they were more than enough and that takes courage.

It takes courage to say, "I am believing this for my life but if that is not in Your plan, You are still good."

In closing, it takes a lot of hard mental and emotional work to survive as a human being in this world. So please know, I am so incredibly proud of you and all the effort you have put into existing. But more importantly, you should be proud of yourself.

I love you.

With all the warm love,
  Karsynn

Reflection Questions

How am I really and truthfully doing at this moment?

_____

_____

_____

_____

_____

_____

_____

_____

_____

_____

_____

_____

_____

_____

_____

_____

_____

_____

_____

_____

Am I bringing forth the most honest and open parts of me that I desire in another?

_____

_____

_____

_____

_____

_____

_____

_____

_____

_____

_____

_____

_____

_____

_____

_____

_____

_____

_____

_____

If I knew my days were coming to an end, what is one thing I hope they take from my life?

_____
_____
_____
_____
_____
_____
_____
_____
_____
_____
_____
_____
_____
_____
_____
_____
_____
_____
_____
_____
_____
_____

Finish this sentence… If I had the courage to tell you, I'd say….

_____

_____

_____

_____

_____

_____

_____

_____

_____

_____

_____

_____

_____

_____

_____

_____

_____

_____

_____

_____

_____

_____

_____

_____

About the Author

I, Karsynn, have a heart for people. As my family and I grow and continue to grow we are realizing that the only thing that matters is that we as human beings walk in tandem with one another as a reminder that no matter what we face, we are never alone. I am curious about life.

I am curious about each person's walk of life, and I am curious to see all that is in store for you and me.

9 780578 340142